leather on willow

*A Collection of Amusing Stories and Pictures
from The World of Cricket*

Published 2005 by arima publishing

www.arimapublishing.com

ISBN 1-84549-040-1

Printed and bound in the United Kingdom

Typeset in Palatino 12/14

arima publishing
ASK House, Northgate Avenue
Bury St Edmunds, Suffolk IP32 6BB
t: (+44) 01284 700321

www.arimapublishing.com

ALL PROFITS FROM THIS BOOK WILL GO TO HELP REBUILD
GALLE STADIUM, SRI LANKA

To Dympna and Katy with all my love XX

A big thank you to Wendy Swan for the proofing and ideas, Andy Clark for getting the stories and pictures to me against all technological odds, Big Harvey for all the stories and buying me a beer in Jo'burg, Andy Lulham of The Mighty Greys, Matt Thacker at 'All Out Cricket', James Holmwood for all the additional contributions, Cridler for letting me pinch some of the Wavey Navy pictures, Neil Jones for the great pictures and everyone else who contributed – you know who you are!

"The sublime waste of an entire day, doing something with no redeeming purpose whatsoever"

Anon (Courtesy of Lew Maton, England)

The Sky stump-cam theft. Colombo 2001.

Many of us were in Colombo in 2001 to watch England's superb, against-the-odds series win. Although the celebrations after the third Test will linger long in the memory, some of you may remember the hoo-ha that ensued when it became apparent that in the excitement at the end of that final game, someone had stolen one of the stump cameras from the pitch and had run off with it. Ten thousand pounds was the figure being bandied about and the TV production company staff were going frantic.

While in Sri Lanka for the Test series in December 2003, the editor bumped into a guy with an interesting story to tell about that previous Sri Lankan series.

Back in 2001, Scott Henderson had been at the second Test in Kandy with a group of other guys. One of them (we shall call him "XXXX") was desperate to get a stump that had been used during the game, in order that he could give it to his cricket-mad father back home.

Unfortunately the police presence at the Kandy Test was bordering on the ridiculous. Their presence seemed to build up throughout the Test and by the time the fascinating game ended in an England victory, there was an impenetrable ring of khaki uniformed officers, many with hungry looking Alsatians, straining at their leads and barking from slavering mouths, surrounding the whole outfield. XXXX decided that he didn't wish to have his limbs bitten off while attempting to get a stump, but vowed to get one at the final Test in Colombo.

And so, a week later, the winning runs were struck at the Sinhalese Sports Club and England won a famous series. The place went bananas. There were at least five thousand Brits in the ground, many of whom wanted to get out onto the pitch. The unfortunate thing about the SSC is that the outfield is surrounded by a low wall. On top of the wall there is fencing which has particularly nasty spikes on top. The whole thing stands six feet high. However, due to its age, in places one or two spikes are missing and a careful leg-up and leap over can be managed without too much fear of nasty flesh founds.

One such section of fencing had been found by XXXX, whose group had been watching the game from the sun-drenched bank in front of the huge scoreboard at midwicket. As the end of the game approached, XXXX was ready. One foot was on the wall and he watched intently through the bars of the fence, ready to clamber over at the appropriate moment. XXXX was really pumped up after being thwarted in Kandy and the egging-on from his mates made him all the more determined to secure a stump that had been used in the Test itself. A poxy six foot spiked fence wasn't going to worry him.

XXXX waited as England got closer to the required score and as soon as the winning runs were struck he hoisted himself up and over the fence and sprinted towards the pitch. He was one of the first onto the outfield, which meant that he was an obvious target for the patrolling police. He skilfully sidestepped three or four of them and grabbed the first stump he got to. As he turned to go back the way he came he could see that by now there were many more people on the outfield, which made it easier for him to avoid the police. He found his way off and back over the fence to the safety of his impressed companions. XXXX spent the next five minutes holding the stump aloft like Excalibur much to the delight of his chums. It didn't take long for someone to point out that he'd managed to pinch the stump with the camera inside. This had been totally unintentional, but it was pointed out to him that these were worth about ten thousand pounds and this would be seen as a serious offence.

As soon as Sky found out that their precious piece of equipment had gone missing, they got onto the police and demanded that it be retrieved. It was, after all, the police that were meant to have been guarding the outfield in the first place.

Sure enough, the police turned up on the bank and didn't have to look very hard. They soon spotted XXXX surrounded by a throng of onlookers and were quick to apprehend him.

The police announced that they were going to take the stump-cam back to Sky, but XXXX protested, saying that he hadn't intended to take the wicket with the camera in it, but had snatched it by accident. XXXX insisted that he wouldn't give up his prized possession unless he too could see Sky, apologize to them and swap the stump-cam for a normal stump.

The police agreed and led XXXX away. Scott says that the last he and the others saw of XXXX is when he disappeared amongst a throng of officers, clutching his prized stump for dear life.

Scott and the rest of the crew missed most of the historic celebrations going on in front of the England dressing room as they waited for XXXX and eventually went to look for him when he didn't return. The police weren't giving anything away about XXXX's fate and Scott admits that he feared the worst.

It later transpired that the police had decided to take a route that involved going outside the ground. As XXXX was led along the street in the baking hot sun, he began to think that perhaps Sky wouldn't be willing to strike a deal. Even if they were, they'd be unlikely to have another actual match stump to do a swap anyway. The more XXXX thought about it, the more he felt uneasy. All that effort, all that excitement could all go down the pan. XXXX began to think about making his escape.

By chance he spotted a tuk-tuk waiting for business at the side of the road. Quick as a flash, XXXX sprinted towards it, jumped in and shouted at the driver to drive as fast as he could. As they sped off, XXXX looked back down the dusty street, half expecting the policemen to have jumped into similar vehicles and be giving chase in Bond-film style. XXXX was surprised and relieved to see them standing shrugging their shoulders and scratching their heads. As the political situation in Sri Lanka was still somewhat unstable at the time, they probably had more to worry about. Nevertheless, XXXX made sure he was dropped off round the corner from his digs in case the driver was subjected to later questioning.

Scott and the rest of the party got back to their lodgings some time later, not having a clue what had happened to XXXX. When they found him sitting on his bed waiting for them, the excitement rose and everyone was desperate for the full story, asking "What happened? What happened?", "Did you get arrested?" and "Where's the stump?"

For a moment he stayed silent and then, slowly and deliberately stood up, reached under his mattress, pulled out the stump-cam, raised it to his lips and kissed it like you might kiss any hard-earned trophy.

Scott says that he and the rest of the guys cheered with jubilation and XXXX was immediately accorded hero status. Before long, they were all in the nearest bar and XXXX didn't have to buy a beer all night.

Later, XXXX kept to his word and presented the stump-cam to his father, but not before he had mounted it on a plinth with an inscribed plaque.

It now sits proudly on XXXX's father's mantelpiece in a terraced house in an English south coast port.

So next time you see the TV engineers coming on to the field of play as the game draws to a close and replacing the stump-cams with traditional all-wood stumps, you'll know the reason why.

The above article first appeared in the Corridor of Uncertainty, issue seven (December 2004).

Andy Clark, England.

Once again the old woman is following the Saffie team. The round-headed, untamed kitchen animal, i.e. the husband, is left at home to look after the tame animals.

After a long flight from Johannesburg to Heathrow, we then took the bus to Gatwick Airport and then the long flight to Barbados. After clearing customs, it was on another plane to Grenada.

Being addicted to Coca Cola, I completely forgot to take a glass of Coke to the hotel room with me. Being tired from flying these things seem to slip an old bag's mind. Anyway, come the next morning I get up only to find no Coke in my room to drink. I got dressed in a pair of shorts and T-shirt and off I went. To top it all, I will not qualify for the Ms World Contest as I have the skinniest legs on Earth - even a centipede has better legs than me.

After walking the streets, looking for some open shop that might sell Coke, I stop a bloke and ask him very politely "Do you know where I can find some Coke?" This bloke takes one look at the old woman, takes a couple of steps back and says "Hey Mon, no Coke here, no Coke here". Still not realising what the problem is, I carry on my search for the illusive Coke. I must mention that this was at about 5 in the morning.

After about two hours - and still no Coke and getting the same looks and answers from many people, I decide to head back to the hotel with the hope that I might get a glass of Coke from the barman only to find that the bar isn't open. Now how stupid can you be.

As I walked into the breakfast room, I stood in the doorway and said to Bev and Andy and some other friends "Well, Hilda has just made an ass of herself on the streets of Grenada". I told them what had happened and fortunately the barman was there and the next minute a glass of Coke appeared. Nothing ever has tasted as good as that glass of Coke.

I knew that both the Saffie and West Indies team were staying in the same hotel, but didn't realise that the West Indians heard what I had said. The next minute this huge dark hand appears on my right shoulder and a voice says to me "In future, ask for Coca Cola, because here on the islands 'Coke' has a different meaning." I looked up and it was Carl Hooper, the captain. Well, I was completely gob-smacked.

One lesson learnt - Coke does have a different meaning.

Hilda Randall, South Africa

****

Cairns on 94 at Taunton against Somerset and he smashed a six into the river and everyone laughed!

Andrew Knight, England

An Englishman Abroad....

Before ....

And After ....

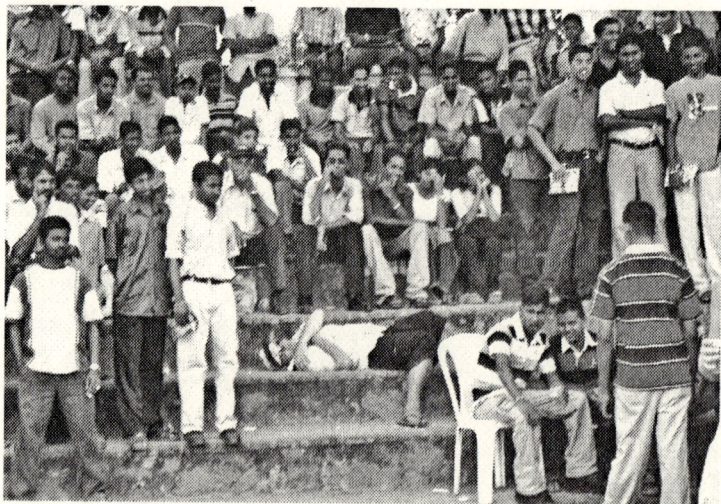

'Sell By', England - Sri Lanka v England, December 2003

SLEDGES

These are some of the more memorable sledges from around the world of cricket. The names of 'The Sledger' and the 'The Sledged' are often interchangeable. Any purists or people of a nervous disposition should look away now....

1.Rod Marsh & Ian Botham:
When Botham took guard in an Ashes match, Marsh welcomed him to the wicket with the immortal words: "So how's your wife & my kids?"

2. Robin Smith & Merv Hughes:
During a 1989 Lords Test, Hughes said to Smith after he played & missed: "You can't f***ing bat".
Smith to Hughes after he smacked him to the boundary: "Hey Merv, we make a fine pair. I can't f***ing bat & you can't f***ing bowl."

3. Merv Hughes & Javed Miandad:
During a 1991 Adelaide Test, Javed called Merv a fat bus conductor. A few balls later Merv dismissed Javed:
"Tickets please" Merv called out as he ran past the departing batsman.

4. Merv Hughes & Viv Richards:
During a test match in the West Indies, Hughes didn't say a word to Viv, but continued to stare at him after deliveries.
"This is my island, my culture. Don't you be staring at me. In my culture we just bowl."

Merv didn't reply, but after he dismissed him he announced to the batsman: "In my culture we just say f*** off."

5. Ian Healy & Arjuna Ranatunga:
Healy's legendary comment which was picked up by the Channel Nine microphones when Ranatunga called for a runner on a particularly hot night during a one dayer in Sydney... "You don't get a runner for being an overweight, unfit, fat c***!!!"

6. Shane Warne & Daryll Cullinan:
As Cullinan was on his way to the wicket, Warne told him he had been waiting two years for another chance to humiliate him.
"Looks like you spent it eating," Cullinan retorted.

7. Glenn McGrath & Eddo Brandes:
After Brandes played & missed at a McGrath delivery, the Aussie bowler politely enquired:
"Oi, Brandes, why are you so fat?"
"Cos every time I f*** your wife she gives me a biscuit," Brandes replied.

8. Ricky Ponting & Shaun Pollock:
After going past the outside edge with a couple of deliveries, Pollock told Ponting:
"It's red, round & weighs about 5 ounces."
Unfortunately for Pollock, the next ball was hammered out of the ground.
Ponting to Pollock: "You know what it looks like, now go find it."

Bunny Haka

Doing the 'Bunny Haka' – Headingley, England – England v New Zealand, June 2004

****

I was scoring and playing (just - at no.11) for my village team Escley, in deepest west Herefordshire, against local opponents Ewyas Harold at their ground, effectively a large municipal playing area with swings, football pitches, play areas and so on. We were batting.

It was a Sunday afternoon (2002 I think) and a few of the local boys had clearly had a few at lunchtime and were "playing" in their cars being silly devils, far from where we were playing our match, around the children's play areas.

One of our lads knew these boys and, as they had yet to bat, joined in and though things never really got out of hand we knew that one of the locals had bumped his car into a child's swing (unoccupied) and an angry passer-by or parent had called the police.

By this time our "yob" had returned and gone into bat for us. 10 minutes later a policeman arrived on the scene asking to speak to Fred Jones (I make that name up, of course!) and came to me as the scorer thinking I might know where he was.

"Well, out in the middle batting" I said.

"Can't help that" he said, "I want a word now".

And the upshot was scorebook recorded "Fred Jones retired; helping police with their enquiries".

Chris & Alison, England

****

We once had a firm's cricket match against another local firm. We had someone who wanted to take part but couldn't get in the team so he was made our umpire.
We bowled first and, in the opening over, the opening batsman clearly got an edge. Everybody went up in the loudest of appeals.

"Not Out", said the umpire immediately in a firm response. At the end of the over, the disgusted bowler collected his sweater from the umpire and said,

"Why didn't you give the batsmen out? You could hear the contact clearly?"

"Yes, you certainly could," said the umpire, "but I couldn't give him out as he had only *just* tipped it!"

Tom Blinks, England

The Beer Stack

(Soon to be introduced as an event at the 2012 Olympics)

Here, the English team attempt the legendary '50 pint tower'

Old Trafford, England – England v West Indies, August 2004
(Neil, England)

****

I was watching a low level club match many years ago when the batsman skied the ball high, high into the air. The batsman and the non-striker both ran looking up at the flight of the ball; the batsman with his mouth wide open. They met in the middle at such a pace that the batsman's teeth went into the non-striker's cheek with such force that he had to go off to hospital for stitches and played no further part in the game. As the ball was cleanly caught, it meant that both batsman were out off one ball!

It is said that, on another occasion, a batsman was struck by a fiercely fast rising ball and laid out; the next man in fainted at the sight of the blood and couldn't bat, the next man flatly refused to go in and face that bowler on that wicket and the next man wasn't padded up in time and was declared out. I don't know whether that story is true or apocryphal.

John Glasgow, England

****

Roly Jenkins was asked to write a chapter in a book entitled 'The Young Cricketer on the Art of Spinning'. When Middlesex came to Worcester (I think in 1947), R W V Robins went up to Roly and said

"Jenkins, your piece on spinning was very good. Who wrote it for you?"

To which Roly replied, "Who read it to you, Mr Robins?"

John Pugh, England

As a young lad of some 14 or 15 years, I sat on the old wooden benches at the New Road End (Worcestershire) and was shortly joined by an elderly lady who emptied her bag and commenced knitting.

After about 45 minutes of play she turned to me and asked,

"Who are the visitors today?"

John Cooper, England

****

A few years ago my family and I set off early for a Holiday. We were traveling through the countryside near Malvern in Worcestershire. The time was around 6:00am when my mother exclaimed in a very strong Brummie accent,

"It's very early for them to be playing cricket".

After quizzing her for 5 minutes we realised that perhaps she should consider a visit to the opticians when the holiday was over as what she was actually looking at was a herd of cows in a field!

Martin Hanney, England

****

I was born and bred in Kidderminster, Worcestershire, not far from the cricket ground on Chester Road. Near one side of the boundary runs the Birmingham to South Wales railway line. There is a well known (and perhaps apocryphal) local story that one day a batsman hit a six over the top and the ball supposedly landed in the wagon of a passing freight train and was found three days later in a steelworks yard some 100 miles away in Newport !

David Pagett, England

****

The incident in question took place when I was umpiring a typical village green cricket match –

Bowler bowled, batsman swished and missed. Ball travelled BETWEEN the stumps and so surprised the keeper that he didn't react and the ball sped to the boundary.

"Howzat?", screamed the keeper.

"What are you appealing for?" asked the umpire.

"Bowled!", keeper replied.

"I can't give him out as the bails are intact"

"But he should have been out if the wickets had been placed properly."

"So they should have been narrower. They were not and the bowler failed to take advantage of this fact - he can't have it both ways."

The batsmen now had his say...

"As I am clearly not out I am claiming 4 byes as the ball reached the boundary!"

The umpire, now the butt of hilarious comments, replied

"Gentlemen, we will reposition the stumps and have that ball again."

Honour being satisfied that ball was rebowled and the batsman dutifully prodded it back to the bowler. Teatime was as good as ever.

David Miller, England

****

I am afraid that I cannot verify this story, so it is little more than folklore, but a friend told me that he went to Uxbridge to watch Nottinghamshire play Middlesex in a four day (or possible three day) game a few years ago. Mike Gatting was fielding a midwicket.

The batsman chipped one over Gatt's head and he made a pathetic attempt to reach for it, feet barely leaving terra firma. A voice from the pavilion then echoed around the ground -

"You'd've caught it if it had been a f*cking pork pie!"

Alan Saunders, England

I'd moved to Canberra in mid-1985, but went back to Melbourne for the Boxing Day test against India. I was very excited, as I was a teenager going on holidays without my parents for the first time, and looking forward to the cricket.

This match featured a young guy by the name of Steve Waugh, who many tipped for great things, making his debut.

It was also the last time in the baggy green cap for one David William Hookes. He scored 42 in the first innings, but in the second dig wound up with a first-ball gozzie. Fortunately for Australia, rain came and washed out the tail end of the match, meaning India didn't win. Come 4pm on the final day, it was obvious that the rain was not going to let up and, if I recall correctly, the team for the Sydney test had been announced. without Hookes.

After the match had been declared a draw, I was one of the few left at the ground, and after hanging around outside the team rooms for a while, a group of supporters walked across to Jolimont railway station. For those who don't know, the station is en route to the Hilton Hotel, where teams, officials, etc used to stay for the MCG test.

Before our train arrived, we looked up at the pedestrian overpass, and saw three Aussie test cricketers making their way over the bridge to the hotel. I don't remember who two of them were, but I do remember David Hookes. He'd obviously decided to mark his omission from the next test, and the probable end of his career in the traditional Aussie manner. He was having trouble walking, and looked like he'd demolished half a day's output from the Carlton and United Brewery.

I'd heard the news that his test career was probably over, and decided some encouragement for one of my childhood heroes was necessary and my teenage voice sang out loudly,

"ONYA HOOKESY YOU BLOODY LEGEND!"

He looked down in my general direction.

He probably didn't see who'd said it, but he waved, and gave a thumbs up...

I can't think of a more apt way to say farewell, than to repeat it.

ONYA HOOKESY YOU BLOODY LEGEND!

Zat, Australia

****

At the ripe old age of 52 I decided to head for Sri Lanka to watch the ICC Championship Trophy series. The first Saffie match was against West India and I was fortunate to sit with the big shots. I met Sir Vivian Richards - apart from the fact that he is one heck of a tall man, he is a gentleman. Anyway, South Africa won and we were all very happy.

As soon as I got back to the hotel, (I was staying in the Galadari Hotel in Colombo), I was greeted by the staff who said "We saw you on the TV" - what an embarrassment. Of course this Saffie has an obsession with a certain Australian cricketer (who shall remain nameless) and off I went to see the Aussie matches.

About a week later my friend, Beverley arrived and we went to the semi-finals between Aus and India. As everybody knows, Aus lost that match and there were rumours that the Aus team would be moving into our hotel on the Saturday.

Well, that Saturday, Bev and I decided to go to Galle and two Aussies (supporters) decided to go with us. I am completely nuts about elephants and on the way to Galle I saw this elephant walking along the road. I just shouted at our guide to stop the mini van and before anybody could say anything, I was out of the van like a flash and after the elephant only to find that it disappeared. How a huge thing like that could vanish was beyond my comprehension. It was then that I realised that if I took one more step I would be diving head first into a river.

There was my elephant with a couple of more elephants being washed and played with. Bev, with big eyes (after seeing her friend vanish) stood there and had the camera out. I went rushing into the river and had the time of my life playing and washing these gentle creatures. The trainer of one of the elephants told him to pick me up with his trunk and what a wonderful experience that was.

The two Aussies just stood there on the bank of the river and said "Oh, this is going to be a very looooonnnnggg day" and it was.

Galle is a wonderful town. So peaceful and the cricket ground, surrounded by a fort wall, is something that I will never forget. We were allowed to enter the seating area where only the members of the club sit and we took photo upon photo. Unfortunately I have lost the negatives, but if I look hard enough I might find the CD it is on.

As long as I live I will never forget the sheer joy of being in Sri Lanka. The friendly people, the smell of spices as you walk down the streets, riding in the tuk-tuk's. I can still smell the spices as I am sitting here. Needless to say, the Aussie team did move into our hotel and I did get to speak to that certain Aussie player and hence my holiday was a success as from day 1. I will remember Sri Lanka as long as I live.

Hilda Randall, South Africa

****

After running to the middle and pouring out drinks from his tray for the Umpires, a streaker makes a hasty retreat!
Old Trafford, England – England v West Indies, August 2004
(Neil, England)

****

A rat was hiding in my kitchen. I had eliminated all hiding places apart from some jars on a work top. That was where the rat was. I looked for a weapon and the nearest to hand was my old cricket bat. The kitchen door into the garden was open outside which sat an interested cat. Slowly I prodded the jars with my bat. Suddenly the rat made his leap for freedom. I lifted my bat and made contact with the rat just as it reached the ground executing a textbook cover drive. The rat sped a mere 6 inches above the ground straight out of the open door. 'Howzat?' shouted the cat as its jaws clamped around the hapless rat. Maybe my cover drive wasn't as good as it should have been as it was a clean catch.

David Miller, England

****

Suffering the effects that most of us felt after drinking lots of Castle Lager, Aussie Nick was forced to pay a visit to the cubicles of the toilets in the Wanderers Rugby Club in order to clear his system of the large amounts of gas that had built up in his lower digestive tract.

Proceeding to do so explosively, he noted with some relief that the locks on the cubicle doors had been fixed. When he had paid an earlier visit, both had been broken.

Having been about his business, he opened the cubicle door, only to find a bemused woman looking at him. He had wandered into the Ladies by mistake!
Big Harvey, England

My village team in North Sussex, Lower Beeding, used to have a few characters.

There was a burly opening batsman by the name of Geoff Crowther. A very decent player, but a fielder who could best be described as statuesque. Consequently he was invariably stationed at first slip. On one occasion, the bowler found the outside edge and the ball flew low to Geoff's right. To general astonishment, he swooped, Botham-like, to clutch an extraordinary catch just inches off the ground. As we rushed to congratulate him, one of the players asked him how he had been capable of such agility, to which Geoff replied "It was either that or run after it, and I ******* hate running".

The other opener was "Biff" Harrison, whose name amply described his stroke-making. Blessed with a fantastic eye, he took the view that if the ball was there to be hit, he would hit it, even if it was the first ball of the innings. I saw him hit a six off the first ball on a number of occasions. In particular, there was one match where we bowled superbly and dismissed the opposition for 49. Biff decided that overhauling such a modest target would not take long, with the result that the match was won inside 5 overs, with Biff 48*, including 6 sixes.

On another occasion, we were up against a team whose opening bowler was sporting a Middlesex 2nd XI sweater. As the other opening batsman on that occasion, I was a little alarmed as he marked out a run-up that extended almost to the boundary. Biff, however, was unconcerned, pulling the first ball for four. This brought a verbal riposte from the startled bowler, which Biff ignored. Two balls later, and the score was 8 without loss, as Biff smote another boundary, again being subjected to a verbal barrage. Then, on the last ball of the over, Biff took two steps down the wicket and cleared the ropes, at which point the bowler almost auto-combusted. "What the hell do you think you're playing at?" he bellowed, to which Biff replied, as wide-eyed and innocent as you like, "I always go down the wicket to slow medium".

Biff's brother, Fred, was the wicket keeper. A giant of a man with fiery red hair and bushy beard, he was actually a very stylish and correct batsman. On one occasion, we had a 16-year-old playing and it was his turn to do a stint at umpiring while Fred was batting. Sensing that the lad might not be too sure of himself, the bowler let out a huge appeal the first time the ball hit Fred's pads. Sure enough, up went the finger, despite the fact that the ball wouldn't have hit a second set of stumps. Fred was apopleptic, threw his bat away towards square leg and refused to leave the field. In the end, the opposition skipper formally withdrew the appeal, and Fred carried on with his innings. At the same time, our skipper formally withdrew the umpire. It was a good few years before he stood again!

The bowling attack was pretty memorable too. There were the twin brothers, Budgie and Alan Harrison. Budgie came in off a short run, but had the fastest arm you've ever seen, with the result that he was forever surprising batsmen with his pace. Alan was not as quick, but his weapon was unpredictability. He needed a few overs to get a rhythm going, and would often, quite unintentionally, let go a beamer early on, often resulting in a wicket as the startled batsman fended the ball away from his throat. The other strike bowler was Geoff Fry, a barrel-chested left-arm quick, who had to bowl round the wicket because he had the lowest arm of all time. Had he bowled over the wicket, umpires all around the county would have been laid out. He also had the longest follow-through of any bowler ever, finally pulling up about two yards short of the batsman. He never said a word, but just glared at the batsman from an uncomfortably close range. I felt intimidated by him, and I was fielding at cover.

The stock bowler was Tony Ford, whose bowling was steady but unexceptional. The reverse was true of his batting, which was utterly unreliable but occasionally spectacular. He only had one shot - two steps down the wicket and a full swing of the bat. Batting second in one game, we found ourselves 7 wickets down and still more than a hundred runs shy of our target. The pub was beckoning, but nobody had told Tony. It was one of those days (actually, the only day) when everything came off. Suddenly, we found ourselves within touching distance of an unbelievable win, as every swish of the willow made contact and Tony raced to 80*. What then followed was one of the funniest things I have ever seen on a cricket ground. Playing his normal shot, Tony sent another ball steepling towards the mid-wicket boundary, where the fielder took a comfortable enough catch. Elated at having finally put an end to this extraordinary innings, he hurled the ball up in celebration and in so doing, threw it over his head and over the boundary. The umpire signalled six, having somehow construed that the fielder had not had the ball under control long enough for it to be counted as a catch. After several minutes heated debate, in which the umpire remained blithely unmoved, the opposition skipper took his team off the field, never to return. We didn't play them again.

Charlie Hempstead, England

A Zulu dance greets every 4 – Durban, South Africa – South Africa v England, December 2004

****

I came to love the game of cricket relatively late in life - there was no school master who whipped the lads into a frenzy of interest at my comprehensive, no odd uncle who once played in a County 2nd XI and no elderly Major to take me see India ("at the Oval!" - one of my favourite quotes from 'Fawlty Towers'). I became embroiled in the love triangle between me, The Game and The Rest Of the World in my twenties but I was determined that, if I had children, they were to suffer no such depravity in their upbringing. Within a week of my daughter being born back in 1991, I had my wife wheeling her around the boundary in the pram and I was convinced that her first words were going to be 'Daddy duck again'

Alas, I couldn't sustain their enthusiasm, mainly because they had better things to do on a sunny Sunday afternoon than watch me lumber around dressed in funny clothes, or learn new and interesting swear words from my team mates. Relentlessly though, in the way the England selectors continue to pick players with a shorter international future than stinky cheese has in the post, in the last couple of seasons I've tried again. Cycling with my son up to the local club to watch was fruitless, but the arrangements at the County Ground in Hove proved more to our liking (inexpensive entry price and a bouncy castle, among other things).

Now that the seed has been planted, it's all that I can do to stop my pre-teen daughter fawning over her signed photograph of one Sussex player (guesses on a postcard to the Press Office), or to stop my son from accosting anyone wearing cricket clothing and asking him to sign his autograph book (Keith Meddlycott got a bit of a surprise, as he was taking a drink to Ahzar Mahmood at the time). This is now a dangerous fiscal situation, as up until now, only I have had to live with the financial consequences of me being a cricket nut - money I'd normally spend by giving to Mr. Shepherd and Mr. Neame is redirected to the excellent club shop, the ice cream van and the burger bar.

Despite this I do hope that there are others out there like me, who have managed to hook their progeny to this most beautiful of games after almost missing a generation. There will surely be hope for cricket if this new breed of fan come to understand that there are some sports in which the matches can last more than 90 minutes and still be exciting. It helps to get new fans interested if the clubs continue to innovate and develop their facilities and their approach their fan base in the way Sussex has in the last five years.

It may be some time, however, before we hire a bouncy castle for my club side's home matches, although there are usually a fair number of clowns on show.

Andy Lulham, England

The McCheeseburger Challenge

Due to the rain washing out most of the first two days, the sad news about the death of Ben Hollioake and the general state of play, day 5 of the second Test at the Basin Reserve should have been pretty flat. Fortunately someone had noticed that it was a Monday and therefore cheeseburgers were only 90 cents (about 28 pence) at McDonalds, next door to the ground.

So the McCheeseburger Challenge took place on the bank. The rules stated that the whole cheeseburger had to be consumed in front of witnesses. The one who had eaten most by close of play was the winner. A contestant would make his way to purchase his cheeseburgers and come back carrying a brown paper bag. "How many, how many?", the other contestants would cry. His reply ("Two", "Four", etc) would come back and be greeted with "Oohs" and "Aaahs". Contestants then had to consume their whole cheeseburgers (untampered with) in front of everyone else.

Here is the official scorecard kindly provided by the official scorer, Scoop.

Congratulations to Dan on an amazing and tactically superb performance.

MARCH 25 '02.   DAY 5, WELLINGTON, NZ
BARNY
ANNY® McCheeseburger Challenge...

BBC Phil   ⅏
Steffo   ⅏ ⅏
Patch   ⅏ ⅏
Well's Smallest ⅏ I
Dan   ⅏ ⅏ III
Ed   ⅏
Richard   ⅏ II
Fanzine   ⅏ ⅏ II
Mad Dog   ⅏
Biss   II
Scoop   III
Spielberg   I
Ceefax   ⅏ (DISQUALIFIED)
Long Sleeping ⅏ II

(Ceefax was disqualified for attempting to surreptitiously remove gherkins)

This first appeared in issue three of the Corridor of Uncertainty (May 2002)

Andy Clark, England

You wouldn't believe the amount of gear that I have in my cricket bag. I know that some players, both amateur and professional, are obsessive about their kit, but I didn't think I was one of them until I did an inventory the other day. My TARDIS-like holdall has everything in it, from my pads and gloves to a squashed packet of cheese and onion crisps I thought about saving to eat in the pub after a game back at the 2000 season.

Cricket is undoubtedly the one of the more resource-hungry sports in Britain, with the weekend warriors decking themselves out in up to £200 worth of apparel to take to the field. Some firmly believe that the price of their outfit will somehow directly enhance their performance, so that mediocre souls such as myself will habitually purchase all kinds of franchised bats, pads, guards and shoes only to trudge back minutes later to a chorus of hilarity.

The most expensive area of the kit bag is the bat department. It would appear, on the face of it, that there is only so much that you can do with the design of the willow wand. It was like this until 1972 when Gray-Nicolls brought out their famous Scoop (based, believe it or not, on a golf club).

Nowadays, bats have grooves and channels in them, springs and honeycombs down the inside, chucks of wood on the back and bits taken off the shoulder, and in the case of one called the 'Woodworm', modelled on a bat that had to be shaved and sanded after it had literally been eaten away. All of these are claimed to 'enhance' or 'enlarge' the sweet spot on a bat - I can consistently find a 'slog spot' on mine, but this other mythical area I find harder to find than a decent magazine in a dentists waiting room.

There are still bat snobs who will religiously follow their Maker season after season, or professionals who are close to a particular make due to their county. Fearnley are to Worcestershire what Gunn and Moore are to Notts, and Newbery to Sussex, although you can often see who the big players are by the Slazenger in their hand. I also understand that the V600 is the 'weapon of choice' for random acts of mindless violence against marble statues.

The best innovation in cricket kit, as far as I'm concerned, is the development of an athletic support that does more than just that - under shorts that have pockets for all manner of protective gear . Seeing the great Sir Viv Richards batting in a test match one day from square leg I thought to myself "Why is he wearing brown Y-fronts?" until it dawned on me than it must have been the thigh bands of his jock strap. This evil device, and we had one in our kit bag that was horrifyingly combined with an abdominal support for communal use, has got to be the one of the most inappropriate items of clothing you can wear, especially if you have a very small changing room.

Andy Lulham, England

****

****

I once appeared in a six-a-side tournament at Finchley.

Each side had one professional in their side and Michael Holding strutted out to represent a particular team and bowl his solitary over at a clearly useful club cricketer who was completely in awe of the legendary "whispering death".

Before the over began he approached Mikey to tell him how fantastic it was that he has turned out to play, despite the fact that he had retired from first class cricket some five years earlier. Mikey just nodded as the guy gibbered on.

So in comes Mikey off barely two paces and this batsman twats him over his head for four, followed by a "Farmer Giles" pull over square leg for four more.

Mikey is NOT amused and signals to the part-time keeper to go back five yards as he has had enough of this bloke.

Still off two paces he puts in an effort ball, short of a length, which the batsman tries to pull away again but is hopelessly late on it and the ball hits him squarely in the box, doing severe damage to the hapless bloke's tackle.

The bloke had to be carried off in severe pain but it was possible to detect a faint smile on his face and later in the bar, he could be seen dropping his pants showing everybody his swollen "blood orange" balls, boasting that it had been the great Michael Holding who had delivered that painful blow.

This first appeared in issue one of the Corridor of Uncertainty (Decmber 2002).

Neal Foulds (ex snooker professional), England

My most favouritest day ever at a Test Match

Staying over in Manchester the night before and watching Clarky fall asleep whilst still eating in a Chinatown restaurant...offering to help Pieman to the ground with his unfeasibly large and heavy hamper...Pieman's gratitude as Clarky and I staggered under the weight of it saying "Thanks, lads, Yvonne would have really struggled on her own with that."... watching Chalky White amble in and then unleash 90mph fireballs as the Windies are fired out for 157...Clarky and I deciding to make our round a double so that we each had 16 pints of beer balanced on four trays to carry and thereafter a huge brown stripe down the front of our once white t-shirts...watching Atherton walk out to bat on his 100th test and groaning as he walked back out for 1...watching the greats, Ambrose and Walsh, on their last tour of England establish such a stranglehold that England and particularly debutant Trescothick are rendered stroke less...listening to Steve moaning that like he'd always said Trescothick would never, ever, make a test batsman...watching Gary don his radio headphones and settle back with eyes closed and a beatific smile on his face as he listened to the primly seductive tones of bodacious Barbadian commentator Donna Symonds...seeing Courtney catch Nasser on the boundary and then step back over it for 6 and not out...seeing Stewie go to the wicket at 17 for 3 and immediately start to cream the support bowling once the Big Two needed a break...waving Shandforth's 'Leg-bye' banner at every opportunity in a vain hope that we would catch the cameras...watching in awe as The Gaffer went past 50 in under 70 balls...watching Steve thoughtfully suck his teeth as Trescothick continued to show exemplary judgement of length and line in support...eating and eating and eating as we began to understand why Pieman's hamper weighed so much...entering party mode as Trescothick passed 50 to raucous howls of delight from most and a sickly smile from Steve...watching in awe as Stewie climbed into the returning Walsh and Ambrose as the day drew on...standing to be a part of an incredible ovation for Stewart as he completed his ton on his hundredth appearance just before the close, a tribute that went on and on and on...feeling a lump in the throat as Courtney Walsh, having bowled the last ball of the day, sank forward with his hands on his knees, only to raise himself immediately to go over to Stewart and shake his hand, unaffected sportsmanship as greatness was recognised and brilliance acknowledged...hitting a pub and watching Clarky's karaoke performance to REM's 'Losing My Religion'...watching the highlights of the days play on the pub big screen TV followed by an interview with Hussain with the sound turned down and one of the hits of the day playing in the background moving Clarky to say that sometimes Nasser sounded just like Santana...travelling back to the hotel by train as Swalesy fell asleep standing up and strap hanging....deciding we'd all had enough as we got back to the hotel at 9.30pm so we'd just have a night cap in the hotel bar before going to bed......heading back out to find another pub as we decided at 9.45pm to scotch the previous plan....eventually drinking in the hotel bar until 2.30am.....finally going to bed thinking back on all of the above and even on some bits that I'd better not put in, that, all in all, that was just about the best day I've had at a Test Match in my life...

This article first appeared in issue four of the Corridor of Uncertainty (October 2003)

Mark Gretton, England

****

I remember the day I fell in love with Cricket - September 6th 1986. Up until then, it was just a casual on-off relationship. Glances across a village green from a speeding car, test matches and when there was sod all to watch on TV on a Sunday afternoon before snooker and football took over all of the schedules.

On that balmy autumn evening I watched, absorbed, as Sussex, in their one-day pomp, brushed aside Lancashire in the penultimate over of the final of the Nat West Bank Trophy. Colin Wells effortlessly hoicked the ball in to the stands at midwicket and Imran Khan got a marvellous half century. That night, watching Peter West say his goodbyes and Ian Gould's gappy grin on the balcony at Lords, I was in raptures.

The initial lust of that first fumbling enthrallment mellowed into casual interest, and although I began to follow the county of my birth, I paid all but the scantest attention to it. It was not until seven years later when on another blistering cup run did my former love bite back. Chasing an improbable 322 for victory, Dermot-bloody-Reeve (Man of the Match for Sussex in the '86 game) hit 13 off the first 5 balls of Franklyn Stephenson's last over after the studiously speccy Asif Din had matched David Smith's first innings ton.

I would have bet my kidneys on Stephenson bowling us to victory - I cancelled my appointment for my 'I Love Franklyn' tattoo the next day - it would be kinder to say, in reflection, that Dermot batted brilliantly. You'll not get me to say it out loud, though. That night I was inconsolable. That night Cricket showed me who was boss, ripped out my heart and stapled it to a passing bus.

Since then I have worshiped at the Altar of Cricket, from days in the rain at Arundel to flicking through Teletext at four in the morning - I never want to go through the intense pain of seeing Roger Twose chip the winning runs over the infield again. I have ridden the rollercoaster ride over the last five years since the arrival of Chris Adams as club captain - the comings and goings of players, some famously past it, some never really there, but in the last couple of years we are starting to achieve the success that I believe that we so unabashedly deserve.

Unlike the big city teams, we don't have the metropolitan appeal to attract a Shaun Pollock or a Darren Lehmann, nor do we have the bucolic charm to entice a Glen McGrath or a Shane Warne, but in Murray Goodwin have an overseas player of true class. This, allied to a balance of talented players both young and old, from the county and outside, the team has started to earn much more respect in the eyes of the supporters and media. More triumph and recognition is surely only round the corner.

Pass me the Yellow Pages - I might just get that tattoo done after all

Andy Lulham, England

****

The Cricket Establishment is still in shock about the introduction of coloured clothing in the one-day arena, but as we all know, it is nothing new, and nothing to be scared about. An article in by His Wordship ChristophSir Martin-Jenkins in 1993 revealed that there are many lithograms of players in coloured shirts from that era, and touring sides were known to wear stripes or polka-dots. More recently, every amateur cricket will have played in a team where one of their number considers 'whites' to be grey-marl jogging bottoms, or even knee length khaki shorts.

Kerry Packer brought the coloured kit to the television in his 1970's World Series, and to be honest the only thing that kept me going through those years of the West Indies in the pomp was the really naff clothes they had to wear. The Aussies got yellow and green, the Kiwi's grey, England got blue, but poor old Windies got what looked, on Channel 9's coverage, like chocolate brown and pink slacks. I was honestly surprised that Huggy Bear didn't open the batting with Desmond Haynes some days.

While we're on the subject of slacks, why is it that the manufacturers of cricket clothing insist on making trousers that would have looked naff when the Dooleys topped the charts? The seams on my trousers must be sewn in with industrial grade trawling nylon, they get snagged to flip on the brambles that surround every rural ground and produce enough static electricity to power a portable defibrillator. Often, we cannot be sure if one of our bowlers is appealing for a faint edge or has got an electric arc off his trousers during his follow-through.

All that aside, and accepting that cricket has now joined the band wagon that football started with shirt merchandising, I'm happy to go along to the ground and get vocal in my 1993 Hogger Sports canary yellow Sussex shirt (so fetchingly modelled back then by Carlos Remy). I know the design has changed at least three times since that first colourful season, but I live in Crawley, and sports shops up here either think that county cricket doesn't exist, or they assume that we're all Surrey fans. I find that unless a sports shop is within cheering distance of a ground, their stock of equipment only stretches to the aforementioned flares and bats ranging in size from 'novelty' to 'Harrow'.

Maybe I should go in for the Supporters Club raffle a bit more often, or save up for a more recent one. Alternatively, I could go really retro at the next game, and turn up in silver-buckled shoes, a cravat, knee length breeches and a polka-dot, collarless shirt and cap but there's every chance that I may get mistaken for Chris Eubank.

Andy Lulham, England

****

What's in a name? A couple of seasons back the counties decided to spice up the Norwich Union League by adopting club nicknames, and presumably much marketing to go with it. Each side was presented with the dilemma of getting a snazzy name to reflect some aspect of their county, or their history. Some of the name adopted are pretty easy to fathom - Lancashire, for example, are sponsored by an electricity company, so Lightning was their new moniker.

Others, like Leicestershire and Warwickshire got theirs from their club insignia (the Foxes and Bears respectively). Some had more tenuous links - the Royals, presumably after a type of pear, the Steelbacks, after Northamptonshire's association with British Steel (although they could have easily been called the Strikes or, in honour of Dr. Marten's, the Cobblers), and the Outlaws from Sherwood Forest's most famous folk heroes.

Glamorgan, the pride of Wales, chose the Dragons, rather then the daffodil and Derbyshire picked Scorpions, maybe as an acknowledgement that their batting often has to have a sting in its tail. The remainder of the sides chose names that were associated with some dynamic beast or entity - we have Hawks, Eagles, Dynamos, Phoenixes and Lions - or have some epithet that suggests that they are tooled up or not to be trifled with - Sabres, Gladiators and Crusaders.

That leaves us with just two - my beloved Sharks and the Kent Spitfires. Leaving aside the fact that the only shark that you're likely to see off the coast of Sussex is the Basking Shark, a piscine beast that filters a 50 metre swimming pool through it's mouth every hour to extract it's planktivorous diet, I'm rather proud of my county's Sharks nickname, and mascot - the truly scary Sid. He's a smooth-headed, seven foot monster with goggly-eyes, enormous teeth and no trousers - much like Bernard Bresslaw in the Carry On films.

Last but not least we come to my Home Counties neighbours, the Spitfires. Their name is said to reflect their association with the Air Force Squadrons based in the South East during World War II. My dictionary says that a spitfire is a person with a fiery temper, so let's hope that all we get is fisticuffs in the middle in any disputed umpiring decisions, rather than a lone fighter plane strafing the opposition's balcony.

The Spitfires were the last of the Norwich Union League's teams to get their name, and even launched an appeal to their fan base to come up with suggestions. The season before the poor lads had come second in a couple of competitions, so I wrote in with the Kent Bridesmaids, and the slightly more obscure Kent Waltons, in honour of the World of Sport Wrestling commentator. I don't blame them for overlooking me, but I will be watching the skies if we're in the same division next season.

Andy Lulham, England

****

The final curtain, the last days of the season and thoughts turn to the winter and for addicts of the truly beautiful game. With the best coverage sold off to satellite, paupers like me are consigned to get out the slide rule to compute when the best time to turn on Teletext or tune in to TMS. OK, so nowadays we have the internet to watch games unfold, thanks to the frantic typos from the CricInfo ball-by-ball scorers but it isn't much fun sitting at the PC with a six pack and a suicide bag of cheesy puffs at four in the morning or six in the afternoon depending on where the action is coming from.

My club had a fantastically successful season. Win, lose or draw there has never been a better spirit or craic in the side. These memories will have to sustain me through the winter in the times when my wife hides the TV remote control or the children steal the batteries out of my radio to power their Gameboys. The winter tours are the only time when I habitually scour any newspapers (and the tabloids) just for a sniff of a scorecard.

The only thing worse than this is the torture of being on a continental holiday and paying four times the face value for four-day old copies of the broadsheets to find out that the Headingley Test has been washed out without a ball being bowled. This year in Italy, the only papers I could get hold of were 'Die Welt' and the 'Herald Tribune' – I bought them anyway in the desperate hope of finding news of how England were limbering up for the Natwest Trophy (I guess the Wall Street Journal may have been a better bet).

Like an addict in cold turkey, I braved the local cyber café and was introduced to the perils of the Italian language version of Internet Explorer. Disaster struck when my money ran out just as I got onto the BBC sports site. The spotty teenager from Strasburg sitting on the adjacent terminal now has quite a few new words to take back to try in front of his English teacher.

Some of the guys in my club are going out to the Caribbean this winter to take in a few of days of the Tests or the One-Day Internationals. Almost exclusively, it'll be those without families, mortgages or a sensible attitude to fiscal matters (or all three). To say I'm envious would be an understatement in the same league as "that Mushtaq bloke can turn the ball a bit". Not only are they travelling to parts of the world that I would chop off any non-essential body parts to visit, but the spawny gits are effectively bridging the gap between now and next April when the English season is gearing up again.

One day, when the children have grown up and flown the nest, I may be able to persuade my darling spouse that we deserve a leisurely holiday on a paradise island – Sri Lanka would be good, so long as it coincides with the Columbo Test. If not, then at least the kids won't have nicked the batteries out of my radio.

Andy Lulham, England

At the Centurion SA v England Test, the beer tent at the rugby club where we were sheltering from a torrential thunder storm was hit by a freak gust of wind, strong enough to flatten a large tree in the car park, crushing two cars.

The instinct of most people (myself included) was one of self-preservation - namely to make for the exit, ready to hit the deck should the tent be torn from its moorings. It was quite a substantial structure, and should this have happened, serious injuries or worse could have resulted.

There was one person however whose approach was rather different. Our Linz vaulted athletically over the bar in order to prevent the fridge containing all the beer that wasn't Castle from toppling over with catastrophic results for the important contents. By this selfless act of bravery, he ensured that thirsty England fans continued to have a supply of something at least half drinkable for the rest of the game.

What a hero !

Big Harvey, England

****

I was once watching a game of cricket at my local club, and a batsman tried to play a front foot shot to the cover boundary, but he missed the ball completely. Not only was he bowled out, but somehow he managed to hit the back of his knee with his bat, and totally did in his kneecap.

Chris, Bradford, England

Planning for the last Ashes tour was already a 24/7 activity even before the ACB decided, three months after switching the Perth and Adelaide Tests, to tell everyone. The result was that many folks were stranded in the wrong place, while many others, like myself, were out of pocket by hundreds of pounds. The fact that I had been planning to head into the South Australian outback to see the solar eclipse on December 4th didn't help. That meant an extra flight to pay for.

Some wouldn't have bothered to argue the case with the ACB. Those of us who did were ultimately rewarded when they accepted they owed us, and hence both I and the ubiquitous Dave Hill were left with a promise letter to show when we reached the WACA for free tickets to the first four days play. Not complete recompence for the biggest balls-up since the world juggling championships, but it made the effort worthwhile. Naturally, they still managed to send a letter saying it was three days, before I managed to get confirmation that it was four. I had an envelope stuffed with various correspondence when I set off down under.

Dave, who Prince Harry had nominated as honourary president of the Barmy Army, made arrangements for us to meet in Perth the day before the Test. True, the photo he supplied was slightly out of date, what with him no longer wearing glasses after laser eye surgery and being about to shave off his moustache, but at least I had his mobile phone number and a rendezvous point. What could go wrong?

Of course, once I reached Perth and tried to ring him I found that the mobile number was wrong. Still, we did have the rendezvous at Perth bus station.

It was at this point I discovered Perth had two bus stations.

So we didn't meet that night. Never mind, there were still plenty of days.

So it was that on Day 1 of the Test I showed up at Gate 3, as instructed on the letter. The steward took one bemused look at the letter, and sent me to gate 6.

Gate 6 sent me on to Gate 8.

At this point I swallowed a fly and almost choked on it.

Gate 8 did not have my tickets, but they had a big idea...go to Gate 3.

Meanwhile the Test match started.

Back at Gate 3 I argued my way into the WACA offices, where the people who obviously weren't in charge had no idea about the tickets. One man in a blazer promised to sort it out soon, and in minutes I was given a private box pass.
A happy ending? Not quite...

Up in the box, which was otherwise occupied by two other English people, a couple of Aussie women soon joined us. They too had not received their complimentaries. The blazered man promised he'd find all the missing tickets and be back with them later. He was never seen again.

Those who were there will remember the dismal batting display that saw England crash to 185 all out. Towards the end of the debacle I made my way towards the Barmy Army on the grass bank, not spotting Dave and having no idea what he now looked like anyway. Having been reminded to get back down to go to the hockey at the end, I was off back to the box when the innings ended.

When I got back six male acquaintances of the Aussie women had entered the increasingly crowded box. Being locals, they were naturally somewhat enthusiastic about the performance of Justin Langer. There was not a shred of diplomacy about me as I gave him endless stick.

At first all went the Aussies' way as the ball flew to all parts, but that changed when Langer went for a foolish third run. As Rudi Koertzen signalled for the replay I knew he was out. The sheer horror on the faces of the local's surrounding me had to be seen to be believed, and my celebrations as the replays confirmed the wicket left them staring coldly at me. Calling their hero a dopey pillock (and some other things) had the effect of transforming the Aussie blokes into six Muttleys, all muttering and giving me the evil eye as they left soon after, not exactly my friends for life.

The two ladies stayed, while England's bowlers were bludgeoned round the park. Hayden, suffering from piles and batting like a man in a hurry to get his Preparation H before the chemist closed, was out hooking. Ponting and Martyn, however, saw Australia past the hundred in only the 15th over.

It was at this point, with stumps approaching, that the older Aussie woman announced they had to go.

"We've got to go and meet Justin", she said.

Justin??? Surely not. My blood froze.

"You know Justin Langer?" I asked.

She looked at me, her expression half smiling, half withering...

"I'm Justin Langer's mother."

Charlie Britten, England

Charlie Britten - Galle, Sri Lanka – Sri Lanka v England 2003

The great Essex joker and slow bowler extraordinaire Ray East did many amusing things in his time. Perhaps one of the funniest was on a slightly slow moving day's play when said gent found himself adrift in the outfield. He noticed a bike propped up against the boundary fence. A wicket fell - bringing with it a left hand/right hand batting combination - and Easty was finding the effort of sprinting from one side of the ground to the other, as required by the captain, a wee bit much. The next thing the crowd noticed was East speeding across the outfield on the bike giving out a joyous whoop!! ... never one to hold back, that Ray East.

Gail, England

Travelling in Pakistan

When you support the football team originally named St. Jude's, after the Patron Saint of Lost Causes, it's always tempting to leave England in November and follow the anticipated misfortunes of the national cricket side. Once the time off work has been successfully negotiated, all that is required is a return air-ticket, visa, insurance, jabs and tabs and enough money to sustain you for a month or so. Throw in a spirit of adventure and before you know it, you're scratching your head outside Lahore International Airport.

I'd expected a rugby scrum of eager taxi drivers, each determined to coax me into his own particular cab, take me to a friend's overpriced hotel, in an area I didn't want to go to and charge me the equivalent of a week's wages for the privilege. Actually no-one approached me for 5 minutes. I ended up standing in the middle of a Car Park muttering "Taxi" to anyone who walked by not carrying a suitcase. Eventually I met Asif, who said simply "Welcome to Pakistan".

His suggested fare was only half of what I had been prepared to pay and as we set off into town I was feeling relaxed and confident. Asif explained the reason the taxi was relatively cheap was due to the fact that he stood to make decent money from the manager of whatever hotel I chose to stay at, so why risk losing the customer in the first place. He suggested that I pick two or three places, and once I had made my choice, to bargain very hard for the cheapest price possible.

I settled for the luxury suite in the Hotel Bakhtawr. The initial bout of bargaining reduced the price by half from a starting point of Rupees 2,000. Tea was provided and I came up with the offer of Rs 900 (£12)a night, so long as I stayed at least a week. The manager feigned disappointment, claiming he'd only make a couple of hundred rupees profit after tax. "Well my friend," I replied. "You'll make nothing if I go somewhere else." A little grin appeared on Asif's face as the manager finally accepted the deal.

One learns quickly in Pakistan. There are no fixed prices. Two individuals are involved in a transaction and as long as both are happy with the eventual outcome, no-one has been unfairly treated. Islamic societies do not accept 'interest' and other capitalist wheezes to 'legally' overcharge people. Most purchases have to be negotiated and profits and savings are accrued according to one's skill in such matters.

Most western visitors to Pakistan will argue to save10 pence over a taxi journey, but will happily pay £10 too much for a hotel room. We have been conditioned into thinking of taxi drivers as a bunch of rogues and hotel managers as good upstanding citizens. Fortunately I live in South London and I've never seen a taxi.

Having arrived only two days before the start of the Test Match, I had to be very careful to get my priorities in the correct order. Hence early the following morning I set off in search of the Department of Excise and Taxation. An "Alcohol Permit" needed to be obtained, for without one what would have been the point of all that haggling for a luxury suite with a fridge. There are no bars in Pakistan and alcohol isn't even available in restaurants. If you're staying in a top hotel, beer can be purchased on room service, to be consumed in the room only, but for those of us on a lesser budget, you have to declare yourself an alcoholic and be issued with your monthly prescription.

It took most of the morning to locate the relevant building. It appeared that everyone in Lahore had some difficulty or other with the Department of Excise and Taxation and the flow of people in and out of the honeycomb, reminded me of London Bridge Station in the rush hour on a Monday morning. After two hours I was close to giving up and returned to the little photocopying shop where I had made extra copies of my passport details before setting off. More tea and the kind man eventually took the sick foreigner on the back of his motorbike and dropped me at the actual building I was looking for.

There were over 90 rooms in the building and I had greeted most of the employees, in most of the rooms, before I was finally given a cup of tea in Room 47. The interrogation began..."And for how long will you be needing this medicine?"

"Well, for as long as I'm here, I suppose. Until the end of the cricket tour."

His face lit up immediately. I had used the magic word. The conversation turned to discussing what Saqlain was likely to do to our batsmen, while he miraculously found a form entitled "PERMIT IN FORMP.R. 2 (NON-TRANSFERABLE)". He made me read it and understand that it was issued under The Punjab Prohibition (Enforcement of Hadd) Rules 1979, to Non-Muslims only. I had been suggesting that Graham Thorpe would take care of Saqlain, but he was far from convinced. "And what else have you brought with you that can deal with spin on our wickets," he teased. I thought for a few seconds before replying "Rain.".

Before stamping and signing the permit, the man wrote something in Urdu in my passport, which presumably put paid to any slim chance I may have had of getting a visa to visit Iran. He explained that there were three "Permit Rooms" in Lahore where I could buy my medicine and that I was entitled to 6 units a month, a unit being a bottle of spirits or a crate of beer. He also told me to study the 9 "conditions to the permit" to ensure it wasn't taken off me at any stage in the future. I thanked him and danced out of the building, much to the amusement of the locals standing patiently in queues everywhere around me.

I took a rickshaw to the Permit Room in the basement of the Avari Hotel, correctly suspecting that I would need a drink, before trying to make sense of the 9 conditions. Twenty half litre bottles of the local Murree beer were purchased for approximately £13 and duly transferred to the Hotel Bakhtawr. Condition No 2 stated that "The quantity of liquor which may be possessed under this permit shall not exceed that specified in the permit". Condition No 4 stated that "The liquor which may be possessed under this permit shall be obtained from the licensed vendor in formL-2".

I never did discover what form L-2 looked like. A very lucid and quite inebriated fellow once confided with me as I was leaving a particular Permit Room, "Half the government forms you hear about don't actually exist. Some are no longer used and others were never printed. If we didn't pay Civil servants to look for forms that don't exist, we'd have to find something else for them to do."

Daniel Byrne, England

The 2004 Rebel Tour

In response to the outrageous decision by the West Indies Cricket Board to impose a massive levy on tickets bought by travelling England fans for England's tour there in 2004, some of us decided to boycott the West Indies series, and travel to watch Sri Lanka v Australia at Galle instead, on our own alternative 'Rebel Tour.' England had recently toured Sri Lanka, and we had enjoyed ourselves there so much that I was almost as excited about going back as I would have been if I'd been going on the tour that I'd been so scandalously priced out of. The emphasis of the Rebel Tour was mainly on enjoyment of some good cricket in the company of Australian and Sri Lankan supporters, but we also thought it was important that we spread the news about the WICB's rip-off to cricket fans from these other countries, who might be affected by such a scam in future.

Despite the lack of any official backing or real organisation on our part, word spread over the Internet and by word of mouth. The turnout of around 60 to 80 'Rebels' was better than anyone had dared to expect, and we made the Sri Lankan newspapers, Radio 5 Live back home, and generally succeeded in getting our message across to our target audiences. As a result of our efforts, should the WICB try the same thing when Australia or Sri Lanka tour there, a good percentage of their supporters and tour operators will have received advanced warning.

So successful was the tour that some people changed their flights, so the Rebel Tour was able to carry on to Kandy, where the numbers were allegedly even higher, and Colombo, where the Rebel Tour flag was displayed prominently enough to be seen frequently on TV.

I hope that no cricket board makes anything like the Rebel Tour necessary again, but we all had a fantastic time and will never forget our couple of weeks in Sri Lanka.

Big Harvey, England

Flash Steve's Drinking Marathon, Galle 2004

As well as being a protest, the 2004 Rebel tour had a strong emphasis on partying. Flash Steve embraced this with his usual enthusiasm, starting on the Lion Beer at 10am on Day 1 of the match. After a successful day for Sri Lanka on the field, and an equally successful day for the England 'Rebels' off it, we were in celebratory mood in the Sydney Hotel at the close of play, and the rafters were raised by some hearty singing, mostly from English voices.

After a couple of hours, those like Flash Steve and Paul, who were staying in Hikkaduwa, and ourselves who were staying in Unawatuna, left to go our separate ways. I think most of us had pretty late nights, but as you will see, our own excesses were put well and truly in the shade by those of Flash Steve.

Arriving at the ground in time for the start of play, I spent a quiet first session rehydrating and watching the cricket. Although I regard it as a perfectly honourable cricket-watching tradition to start on the beer at 10 am, my personal preference is to wait until noon. At the interval, I retreated with some English and Australian supporters to the Galleria, a new bar overlooking the ground, and had a very long, sociable, and beer-soaked lunch in great company.

Returning to the ground, I bumped into Paul.

"Have you seen Flash Steve?" he asked me.

"I think that's him over there by the beer stall. Why?"

"I'm dead worried about him. He hasn't been to bed!"

The implications of this sent shock waves through my very being, rooting me to the spot, and causing my mouth to drop open in a mixture of horror and admiration. In mid afternoon, what kind of state was someone going to be in who had started drinking at 10 am on the **previous** day, had not been to bed, and had by all accounts been on the beer more or less continuously throughout?

We looked across to the beer stall, and sure enough, there was Flash Steve. Amazingly, he was in the company of an extremely attractive young Dutch girl, who seemed to be hanging on his every word. We were reassured that incredibly he still seemed OK.

Even after the close of play, he was still sober enough at around 6.30pm to ride a bicycle into the bar of the Sydney Hotel, hotly pursued by the cycle's owner, and order a round of drinks before dismounting and surrendering his two-wheeled transport.

All good things must come to an end though, and the first rule of sensible drinking is to know when you've reached your limit. By 7.30 pm, Flash Steve knew that he'd reached his, and negotiated a tuk-tuk to take him back to Hikkaduwa. Unfortunately however, Hikkaduwa is quite a long way from Galle, and by the time the resort was reached, the effects of the beer and lack of sleep had caught up with Flash Steve to such an extent that the tuk-tuk driver was completely unable to rouse him in order to find out where he was staying.

The whole scenario could have had a very unfortunate ending, but thankfully for Steve, he awoke early the following morning on the floor of the tuk-tuk driver's house. The fact that the tuk-tuk driver could more easily have left him in a ditch minus his wallet was not lost on Steve, who rewarded the tuk-tuk driver and his family generously, before negotiating the immediate hire of the tuk-tuk on a self-drive basis for the rest of the match. Paul, who remarked that sharing a room with Steve saved a fortune on single supplements, was woken up on the morning of Day 3 by the sound of a tuk-tuk engine revving outside his window. Apparently on their way to the game, Steve even stopped to pick up a fare!

Big Harvey, England

Traveller's Tummy - Dhaka 2003

One inevitable consequence of travelling the world, is that from time to time you will suffer from bouts of a complaint that has various names, one of the politest of which is "traveller's tummy". When I announced to one of my workmates that I intended to go on England's inaugural tour of Bangladesh, he pronounced me mad, and said that he would run a sweepstake on how long it would take me to get the "Helmut Schmidts".

I arrived in Dhaka, and having slept off my jetlag, went out to explore. As I surveyed the scenes of chaos around me, my ears were blasted, and my nose took in the various pungent aromas of Dhaka's commercial area. I could feel my guts starting to liquefy straight away. The following day, I was able to e-mail my workmate to the effect that whoever had drawn 16 hours in the sweepstake was the winner!

Big Harvey, England

Sitting on Harry's Tea - Dhaka 2003

Prince Harry (the Everton-supporting one from Birkenhead) is known to virtually everyone who travels to watch England on a regular basis. In Dhaka we were staying in the same hotel, and went to the stadium together for the first day's play. Although like me, Harry had tickets for the cheapskate's section of the ground, he wanted somewhere prominent to put his flag, and so headed for the posh 'official' Barmy Army section.

I waited patiently at the bottom of the stairs for him to return, but it eventually dawned on me that having blagged his way into the posh seats, he was unlikely to come back unless thrown out. I therefore made my own way up there, told the steward I had a message for my friend, and was in the expensive section myself.

I arrived just in time to see the first ball ever in a Test match between Bangladesh and England, which will be something to bore people with in years to come. Four overs later, the heavens opened, and the pitch was underwater within minutes. It was time for a cup of tea.

Now anyone who knows Harry will tell you that the drinking of tea at a cricket match is an activity to which he is not very familiar. His favourite tipples are Stella and chardonnay, but with Bangladesh being an Islamic country, neither of these was available in the ground. Despite the absence of booze, Harry still managed to enjoy himself, and told me at the close of play that in many years of watching cricket this had been the first time he'd been conscious enough to witness stumps!

It was probably the fact that he wasn't practiced at tea drinking that led him to leave his cup of tea on the seat next to him for me to sit down heavily on. Like most tea in Bangladesh, this stuff was extremely strong, dark, reddish brown, and made with sweetened condensed milk. In other words, the chances of me getting the stain out of the back of my trousers were very slim indeed.

Approximately nil, in fact!

Despite various attempts over the next couple of weeks to shift this evil stain, it stubbornly refused to budge, and there was much giggling at my expense as a result for the rest of the tour.

Big Harvey, England

Overweight Aussie - Brisbane 2002

Much has been made of the obesity epidemic currently sweeping Britain. It is caused by a combination of poor diet and lack of exercise, or in the author's case, excessive quantities of healthy food and good beer! In Australia, with its sunnier climate and the consequent popularity of the outdoor lifestyle, obesity is less common. As you will see though, it is far from unknown.

To poke fun at fat people is unkind, although sometimes it can be justifiable, as in the following case; that of an overweight Australian gentlemen who launched into a decidedly ill-advised foul-mouthed, incoherent, drunken tirade of abuse against the Barmy Army from a couple of blocks away in the stand.

The Barmy Army, pleased that the day's Aussie-baiting had borne fruit, at least in the stands, predictably launched into a chorus of 'Who Ate All the Pies', followed by 'You've Never Seen a Salad'. Someone within the ranks then speculated that the reason for the Aussie gentleman's unpleasant demeanour was that he must be hungry. An immediate whip round was held, and a pizza paid for from the pizza seller, who was promptly sent to deliver it to the person concerned.

As the pizza seller disappeared from view, silence descended, followed by one of those cheers that starts very quietly and gradually rises to a crescendo of noise. The crescendo of noise peaked as the pizza seller emerged into the foul-mouthed Aussie's section and presented him with his cholesterol-laden treat amidst massive cheering and laughter from English and Australian fans alike.

Apoplectic with rage, the recipient flung back the pizza in the direction of those who had paid for it, but this act only completed his utter humiliation. He sat back down in his seat, with only his team's performance on the pitch to console him. We never heard another peep from him all day.

Big Harvey, England

Bus Journey From Hell! – India 2001

My plan had been to spend a couple of weeks travelling around and seeing the sights prior to the first Test in Mohali. Although I'd never been to India before, I knew that it was almost inevitable that I was going to pick up some sort of stomach bug sooner or later. It was simply the timing that was unfortunate. After two weeks of eating exclusively local food in local dhabas and restaurants, I'd encountered no problems whatsoever. Following a western-style breakfast in a backpacker-orientated restaurant in a village outside Manali, however, I began to feel extremely unwell. The fact that I was supposed to be taking an 11 hour overnight bus journey to Chandigargh that night in order to be there in time for the cricket made this decidedly inconvenient, since no way would I be able to travel while feeling like this.

After a particularly violent bout of projectile vomiting though, I began to feel considerably better, and the prospect that I would be able to travel after all was all of a sudden a real one. I hurriedly packed my stuff, checked out of my 75 pence per night room, and got an auto-rickshaw to the bus station. Unfortunately, by the time I reached Manali, I was feeling awful again. My bus was there and had started boarding. Should I get on it or not?

Suddenly, the only thing that mattered was that I needed to be sitting down. I was in a cold sweat, weak at the knees and barely able to stand. At that moment, the bus looked a more appealing option than an auto-rickshaw back to the village.

I boarded, and took a seat next to the window. This was how it came to pass that as the bus departed Manali on a projected 11-hour journey, I was throwing up out of the window. Thank heavens I hadn't chosen one of those super deluxe air-con buses with windows that don't open!

After I'd thrown up everything I had to throw up, I managed to close my eyes and doze for a short while, before I felt the bus come to an unexpected halt. Yes, that's right, it had broken down. After a brief spell of attention with hammers and spanners, the driver departed in a taxi back to our point of origin in Manali to get the necessary spare part.

It seemed as if we were stuck in the middle of the unappealing one-horse town in the Himalayas where we had come to grief for an eternity. I bought some water, drank it, and watched locals setting fire to crisp packets and other assorted malodorous rubbish in order to keep warm. It seemed to be the most popular pastime here. The smell caused me to throw up the water I'd just drunk, so I bought some more.

Eventually we were on the move again.

The bus swerved, bounced, lurched, sounded its horn repeatedly, braked suddenly, and did everything except actually collide with anything. My eyes remained firmly shut until the bus actually did collide with something. There was a brief commotion as details were exchanged, and we were on our way again.

At about 2am we stopped for a break at a dirty, soulless hotel in the middle of nowhere. The food looked so unappetising that it's highly unlikely that I'd have eaten anything even if I hadn't been ill. I noticed with satisfaction on returning to the bus that my own prolific streak of vomit down the side had been joined by several others from different windows.

After what seemed like a fairly short time, we were stationary again. It was still dark, so I couldn't see what was happening. I dozed off again, and when I awoke, we still hadn't moved. Dawn was breaking to reveal an amazing sight. Ahead of us as far as the eye could see, along a winding road clinging to the side of a steep mountain was the mother of all traffic jams. Line after line after line of brightly painted trucks, all prominently displaying the slogan "Use Horn Please!" on the back. The drivers had all taken large boulders from the side of the mountain and lodged them behind their back tyres to stop them rolling back down the hill. Didn't they trust their handbrakes or something? Were they even equipped with handbrakes?

I was feeling slightly better by now, and got out for some fresh air. There were even more vomit streaks down the side of the bus now, some of them looking suspiciously like what had been served up at the hotel we'd stopped at earlier. It all made me feel much less self-conscious about my own previous 'parking of the tiger'.

By the time we finally got on the move, dodging the aforementioned boulders that the truck drivers had neglected to remove, we were running even more significantly late. What had caused the jam? Had something gone over the side of the mountain? Probably.

Once we'd descended from the mountains, it was announced that the bus was going to miss out stopping at Chandigargh in order to make up time. Chandigargh passengers were dumped in a small village to catch the next local bus. Actually, 'village' is being a bit optimistic. It consisted of a pair of straw huts by the side of the road, but at least one of them sold chai!

Thankfully the bus had free seats, and our tickets were honoured, so maybe they'd been expecting us. The couple of hours it took to get to Chandigarh passed uneventfully, save for passing the scenes of a couple of spectacular and quite possibly fatal accidents, one of which had resulted in a bus ending up on its side. Nothing out of the ordinary, in other words.

I arrived triumphantly in Chandigargh seventeen hours after setting off, a mere 6 hours late. My stomach bug had completely gone, and after a good night's sleep I was in fine fettle for Day 1 of the Test.

Big Harvey, England

What a Shambles! – Perth 2002

So impressed was I with the organisation and security at the Brisbane and Adelaide Test matches on the 2002/2003 Ashes Tour, that by the time I reached Perth, I had begun to think that the ability to get things right was an Australian national trait. True, the beer inside the grounds was of such low strength that it was not worth drinking, but having witnessed the behaviour of some of the locals, even on this low strength stuff, the lack of anything stronger was perhaps understandable.

The Third Test at the WACA in Perth, however, was to prove that even the Australian authorities are capable of messing things up big time!

"We do things a bit differently here," Western Australians repeatedly told me. So it was to prove.

I arrived at the ground an hour before the start of play to be greeted by the sight of long queues. Whereas at Brisbane and Adelaide, bag searches were conducted painlessly **inside** the turnstiles, here there was a (completely inadequate) row of tables **outside** the ground. The searches were being conducted so slowly that despite having allowed myself an hour, I missed the start of play. As I entered the ground, it occurred to me that since the only evidence that my bag had been searched consisted of a tag attached to the handle, there was nothing to stop me from heading off to the nearest bottle shop/arsenal and stocking up with as much booze/offensive weaponry as I wanted to. The same thought had clearly occurred to a number of locals, who within a few minutes of getting in were decidedly intoxicated.

"You'll be asleep by lunch" sang the Barmy Army to a couple of young locals on the hill in front of them who'd managed to smuggle in some strong spirits. This prediction proved to be entirely correct, although not before one of them had managed to throw up all over himself.

"Stand up if you've p*ssed yourself" sang the Barmy Army to his friend. Embarrassingly, the young lad obliged, to reveal shorts that were indeed very heavily saturated with urine. It wasn't long before he joined his vomit-caked companion in a state of unconsciousness.

It must have been lunch by the time those who had only allowed themselves a few minutes to get into the ground gained access.

Those unfortunates would have arrived just in time to hear officials from the Western Australian Cricket Association patting themselves on the back, and congratulating themselves over the wonderful job they'd done in refurbishing the WACA. They seemed particularly proud of the 'International Food Court'. I was hungry, so went to investigate. The foods on offer made the stuff available in a typical English ground appear like gourmet cuisine in comparison. In fact, it made the foods available in a typical English white burger van parked in a roadside lay-by appear like gourmet cuisine.

I suppose at a stretch, the food could be described as 'international'. Pizzas - not very nice ones (Italian) - were joined by hot dogs (American), fried chicken (American), and burgers (American). The latter three could be accompanied, if you wanted, by fries (French). It is possible that Chikko Rolls (Australian) were also available, but I didn't like to ask. Anyone who has sampled this particular delicacy will know why.

Outside the ground I met a man who'd been a member for thirty years, but was ticketless. The Association had apparently failed to allocate sufficient tickets to its own members! Understandably the Association were not in his good books.

During the afternoon, things went from bad to worse. At Brisbane, (very professionally) and Adelaide (less sensitively, but reasonably competently), security had been handled by the local police.

Here, security matters were handled by a private contractor. It was quickly obvious that the security firm concerned, or at least the people working for them, had little or no experience of handling this type of event. In fact, most looked as if they were more used to masturbating in front of CCTV monitors than policing sporting events. Every single one of them was heavily overweight. They patrolled the Hill, insensitively ejecting spectators, at least the ones they weren't too slow and unfit to catch, for heinous crimes, such as engaging in friendly banter, and inflating beach balls.

Deprived of their harmless methods of having fun, the locals, many heavily inebriated on smuggled-in booze, began to engage in fistfights amongst themselves. Meanwhile, some of the English supporters were taking advantage of the cooling afternoon breeze known as the 'Fremantle Doctor'. They were holding up plastic bags and releasing them to be blown by the wind around the edge of the boundary. This was not in itself amusing, but the fact that each one was breathlessly pursued by one of the aforementioned puffing, sweating and obese security guards most definitely was!

Although there is no way I would condone such behaviour, the sight of a uniformed Billy Bunter look-alike waddling as fast as his legs would carry him towards a bag that had settled on the grass, only for it to be whisked away again just as he made a lunge for it, had us all in absolute hysterics.

How much did the Western Australian Cricket Association pay for their security arrangements? My suspicion is peanuts. Whatever the truth, they certainly got monkeys!

Big Harvey, England

Memorable moments

There are memorable experiences at every game we go to - plenty of them completely unrelated to the cricket.

Mike's sensational catch on the boundary to win $1000 at the Basin in the Catch A 6 competition was quite wonderful. We'd had a big night at the Vespa Lounge the night before and were watching the game on TV when we realised NZ were going to slog for a bit and then declare. It was a very dull game against Zimbabwe until that point. We got to the Basin and set up camp at Cow Corner. Mike was obsessed with catching a six and mucked up about 10 practice throws that we gave him with the tennis ball. Then Astle got hold of one and smashed it our way - Mike was up, barged a couple of Indian spectators out of the way and took a lovely catch. Later in the day Chris Martin dropped a goober at mid-on off BGK Walker and they had a split-screen showing "the club player on the left, and the test player on the right".

It was brilliant. Another was when Craig McMillan was out for a few beers with us in Taupo during a one-day series. He'd just shaved his head. Two days later on the bank at the Napier one-dayer we demanded he take off his hat and unveil his new haircut. He refused for several overs then we yelled (via megaphone) "If you don't show us your lid we'll tell David Trist [NZ coach] what time you got home in Taupo." The hat came off 1 second later.

Least memorable moments...

Not surprisingly the least memorable things haven't been remembered. Getting told off by the security guards in Wellington at the Caketin and the Basin for yelling too noisily is always ridiculous. They're a mixture of the unemployed and the unemployable - such a marked contrast between their approach and that of the security guards at places like Lord's where the guy keeping an eye on our stand (Adam from Ireland) high-fived us on our way into our seats each day and was just a wonderful chap.

The Beige Brigade, New Zealand

AHMEDABAD

AHMEDABAD is affectionately termed the 'Manchester of the East' by visitors and townsfolk, but to the England fans who arrived in south western Gujarat for the second Test, the similarities between the two cities are few and far between.

Before arriving in the city, few had heard of Gandhi's birthplace, but all were sorely aware of the alcohol prohibition that takes place in this state - which was obviously their main concern. Some Barmy Army Pakistan 2000-2001 veterans were quite gung-ho about their chances of procuring bottles of Kingfisher beer or Director's Special whisky, declaring knowingly that there is booze to be had in every corner of the world, regardless of official, religious or social policy governing the supply of alcohol. They would cite the infamous US prohibition of the twenties, where stills sprang up across every village, town and city in the country. How wrong they were!

For this writer, acclimatization had begun a week earlier, with a strict programme of alcohol reduction at high altitude comprising fitness training, a high-protein diet and intensive counselling by a professional psychiatrist. On arrival, I was confident that the storm would be weathered as long as I took it one day at a time and didn't look too far into the future. Five days isn't too long in anybody's diary, but in a city like Ahmedabad, it feels like a lifetime.

Lack of alcohol was not the only consideration for the tourists, although it did play heavily on the mind in the blistering heat of the open stands. After the precise organisation and excellent facilities of Mohali, one Test prior, arriving in Ahmedabad felt like setting foot in a different world.

The city is not a regular cricket venue, and the Motara stadium does not play host to Ranji Trophy cricket, so the furore of an international match was mighty exciting to the locals, who rarely see tourists and visitors to Ahmedabad.

From first impressions, this was the real India that is often so difficult to find on the well-worn tourist routes of the Subcontinent: a world away from the glitz of Mumbai or the colours of Jaipur. This was an India that has been untouched by the West, and very unfamiliar ground for a gaggle of around 40 Barmy tourists.

Hotel accommodation was quite limited, with a choice between a couple of plush international hotels and a handful of cheap guest houses. For those who chose budget rooms, it was really luck of the draw if the grubby and stained mattresses harboured bed bugs with sharpened fangs. Rooms were dusty and modest and facilities were limited.

All was well, though, because sightseeing and comfort could wait until after the serious business of a Test match, with England one-nil down in the series.

The stadium was a distance away from the crowds and noise of the city centre, way past shanty towns, huge power stations, belching out clouds of noxious gas into the already over-polluted atmosphere, across bridges, through traffic bottlenecks and situated in a bleak, brown outskirt of the city. At first sight, the ground was a sprawling urban oasis of concrete greyness, surrounded by dusty car parks filled with ancient, black two-stroke motorbikes and hoards of hawkers. The police presence was high and security was strict for all entering the stadium.

Most of the England fans took root in an open-air stand at the opposite end of the ground from the towering pavilion. In December, temperatures approaching 30 degrees, this area of the ground was perfect for basking in the sun while taking in the cricket. It also provided a great opportunity to watch an Indian crowd go wild.

Our supporters were easily outnumbered by the police presence, in their khaki army-style uniforms, berets and long bamboo sticks. As the match progressed, more and more coppers entered our stand, to sit in peace and enjoy the cricket.

Towards the end of the third session of the first day, Martin Hegg, Warren's brother, who had come to India to follow his brother's performance with the drinks tray, made a key observation. "Bloody hell! It's Freddy Mercury!" came the cry in flat, Bury vowels, and everybody looked to the entrance of the stand as a well-pressed policeman with immaculately trimmed moustache above a champion set of teeth shimmied up the path between seats. Indeed,

it was a kind of magic as the long-thought-dead Freddy made an appearance in police uniform. As the match progressed, he got increasingly more into the swing of things, to choruses of 'I want to Break Free' and 'Barcelona', and became the fans' favourite piss-take throughout.

For a city famed for its textile industry, Ahmedabad must surely have more weavers than designers. It was almost as if there was a cricket supporter's uniform, embracing thick woolen knit and the colour brown. Overdressing was in fashion: next to the pink exposed torsos of the England fans, the Indians were all wrapped up warm to brave the chill of the Gujarat winter. Few dared to venture from their houses without a thick vest underneath a shirt and tank top, and many took to wearing scarves to keep out the elements.

The cricket during this match was excellent, with fine, attacking captaincy and the reemergence of bodyline, within the rules of the game. There were wonderful innings by White, Trescothick and Foster, who showed how much potential he has for the future, once he's mastered taking the ball on the half-volley. Sachin, as expected, lit the touch paper and set off some beautiful fireworks to a crowd that doubled in size with the anticipation of seeing their hero bat. With his arrival at the crease, every single Indian went potty, surging through the stands, screaming appreciation at the Marathi Bradman and brandishing placards, from bed sheets with painted slogans to small sheets of A5 paper with hand-written comments, all held up hopefully to the cameras in case of a fleeting glimpse for the world to see.

As soon as Tendulkar fell, the crowd had seen enough, and with hours left to play, they swarmed from the ground to leave but a fraction of the crowd. To those used to being told constantly that Sachin is the greatest player in the world, it was obvious that there is much more limited regard for the other players in the esteem of the Indian fans. This leads this writer to feel that there can be little cohesion - resulting in modest success - among the team itself with a hero and ten acolytes in the dressing room. Surely this must have an adverse effect on team spirit that leads to rifts among the players.

The close of play was a dreaded time for many tourists, as leaving the ground amounted to running the gauntlet among the tens of thousands of Indian fans to the rickshaw stand a couple of hundred yards away. It often felt like many people in Ahmedabad had never before seen a Westerner in the flesh, and a sighting would prompt pinching, slapping, touching and shouting, with more and more Indians joining the melee. This writer vividly remembers the close of the fourth day, which necessitated a full-speed sprint amidst some near violent behaviour by a thick curtain of Indians. Once in the rickshaw, we were surrounded by what felt like a mob. Suddenly, the roof of the rickshaw looked, from the inside, like a pendulum, rocking precariously with the force of people attempting to topple it over. Quick manoeuvres by the driver allowed us to escape the crowd and we zoomed onto the road back to the hotel, suffering little more than scratches and seething bad moods.

In all, Ahmedabad was an assault on all senses. The pollution on the wide roads was stifling, particularly in the evenings, and the dirt and dust was choking. The city could never be accused of being green, leafy and beautiful, but there were a number of plus sides that made it all worthwhile.

The standard of cricket was fantastic and the food stands around the stadium served mouthwatering, cheap food. Watching cricket in an Indian backwater was a world away from the sanitized civility of Mohali, with exuberent supporters demonstrating a great deal of passion for their country. All memory of the West was lost for five days, and strong Indian customs took over, such as men often holding hands while walking in the streets, or even cuddling up to each other when seated, holding each other's pinky tenderly.

And even the most alcoholic supporter was able to detox for a short while away from the bottle. Eventually, it was possible to procure beer from government-licensed shops once a permit had been issued, but this was fraught with paperwork and bureaucracy, and this writer managed to secure his weekly allocation of ten beers the night he set off for Bangalore. It felt like a just reward, and, although lukewarm, they went down very nicely indeed.

This article first appeared in issue two of the Corridor of Uncertainty (March 2002).

Richard Whitehead, England

Cliff Booth, Kent CCC Scorer, in conversation with Richard Wiggins

worded by James Holmwood

In 1993 Duncan Spencer was in his first season for Kent having lived in Australia for most of his life and was due to play for Kent 2nd XI at Swansea. The rest of the side told him that if he produced his passport at the Severn Bridge crossing he could have a Welsh dragon stamped in his passport to add to the many stamps already featuring inside his passport. Duncan believed the rest of the side were having a laugh but just to be sure he telephoned his Dad back in Australia to make sure. His father, playing along with the joke, told him he had heard of the dragon stamping and sent his son happily on his way.

The day came to head for Swansea for the game and Duncan packed his passport along with his kit. He was travelling with future England player Mark Ealham and as they neared the tollbooths Mark told Duncan to pass him the passport as the attendant would be on his side of the car. Duncan eagerly passed his passport over waiting to see the new addition to his passport.

Mark drove up to the tollbooth and as the attendant put his hand out to take the toll he was given Duncan's passport. Mark winked at the toll man and said his passenger was an Aussie cricketer over for the season. The attendant took the passport, looked through it and returned it to Mark saying "blooming horrible photo."

Cliff Booth, Kent CCC Scorer, England

The Freddyhouse

A group of England fans, guided by a Welshman called Mad Dog, found a Fred Flintstone Wendy House in a toy shop in Bangalore and clubbed together to buy it. It had a door, side windows, a picture of Fred Flintstone on the front and 'The Flintstones' written on the sloping roof. It was erected in the ground and every time Flintoff came on to bowl the Freddyhouse was held aloft and "There's only one Freddy Flintoff" sung with gusto. It helped Freddy get four wickets, provided shelter from the rain and entertainment for everyone, especially in the local bars.

This first appeared in issue two of the Corridor of Uncertainty.

Andy Clark

I was standing in a game at Tunbridge Wells between Kent and Essex, Essex were batting and Ray East was facing Eldine Baptiste.

Baptiste bowled a full length ball which East jabbed to square leg/mid wicket and in playing the shot he stumbled down the wicket a couple of yards, he looked up at the catcher then at me, shrugged his shoulders and walked off.

This was about 15 minutes before tea and the new batsmen came in and played out time before the break.

At tea East had me and my partner, the late Jack van Geloven, and all of the players in stitches. He claimed he was out to a bump ball and was coming out to bat again after tea. It was as much the way he said it as anything else but we carried on with tea and headed out for the afternoon session.

As luck would have it the first over after tea was from Jack van's end. At Tunbridge Wells the pavilion is directly behind the bowlers arm and all the players walked out in a line and unknown to us Ray East was heading back out to the wicket as he had promised at tea.

He was hunched behind the fielders as they walked out and stood directly behind Jack Van. Neither Jack nor I realised East was there.

The fielders all got in to position and as play was about to restart East tapped Jack on the shoulder.

Jack turned around and almost fell over at the sight of East in his pads and helmet, he then told East to f off.

It brought the house down, the spectators knew what was going on and East slumped off the field, it was a nice bit of humour that sadly you do not see in the game today.

John Holder, First Class Umpire

****

Steve Rhodes the Ex-England and Worcestershire wicketkeeper was one of the first Englishmen to play at the Galle stadium in 1986.

He was a member of the England B side that played an unofficial test versus Sri Lanka at The Esplanade, the previous name for the Galle stadium. Here Steve recollects a moment that stands out for him almost 20 years on from his first game in Galle.

We were playing in an unofficial Test match against Sri Lanka, the previous two tests had seen the two sides cancel each other out and we wanted to win the series.

Bill Athey had scored a superb 180 odd and we were heading into the last day with Sri Lanka eight or nine wickets down but Hashan Tillakaratne was still in and batting well. We wanted to get him out as we fancied our chances of chasing just over 100 in the 20 odd overs that would be left before close.

Syd (David Lawrence) was bowling and came charging in as he always did. Tillakaratne got a big knick on the ball and I dived taking the ball to my right. I had caught the ball on the half-volley but with the pitch and outfield being so dry there was a load of dust flying around and Syd went up appealing for the catch.

I never appealed for the catch but Tillakaratne was f-ing and blinding saying he never got a touch on the ball.

I walked up to him and told him he had knicked it and this infuriated him even more. I then added that the ball had bounced before it reached me and this did not improve the situation.

I ended up inviting him round the back of the changing room when play had finished!.

Steve Rhodes, Ex England and Worcestershire Wicket-Keeper

THE TREVOR MADONDO FAN CLUB

While selling the Corridor of Uncertainty at the Basin Reserve in Wellington during March, the editor got chatting to a fellow named Brandon Clarke, a Kiwi who together with his mates had brought into the ground various items of furniture, a very large parasol and several chilly bins as well as other cricket watching paraphernalia. We got chatting and he told me about the Trevor Madondo Fan Club. Here, Brandon gives an account of its history.

In February 1997 I hitchhiked from Auckland to Wellington to watch the second test between New Zealand and England at the Basin Reserve. This was my first visit to what has become my favourite test ground, and I fell in love with the Basin. I returned for the first Boxing Day test at the Basin, against India in Decmeber 1998. In the lead up to Christmas I suggested to my friend Will that he should come with me this year, and when he said yes, what was to become the Trevor Madondo Fan Club had its second member.

We left Auckland at 3am on the morning of Boxing Day and started the eight hour drive south. As we were working our way through the suburbs of Auckland I spotted an old armchair abandoned on the side of the road and got Will to stop the car and reverse back to it. It was in pretty good condition, so with a little repacking of the car it was in the back seat and bound for five days of test cricket at the Basin too. And so began a tradition that develops more and more flavour each year.

For that Boxing Day test, versus India, it was just Will and I. Him on what has become known as 'The Cricket Watching Chair', and me on a canvas fold out chair. Simon Doull took the first seven wickets to fall on the first day in a spell of swing bowling that was easily the best I've seen until Matt Hoggard's effort at Christchurch this year.

The following year, Will and I returned for the Boxing Day test against the West Indies, and had the privilege to see Matt Sinclair score 214 on debut. A friend of ours from Wellington joined us - and then there were three.

The tradition gathered real momentum in 2000 when a friend of ours returned from living in the UK with her English boyfriend, Ed Garrie. They arrived a week before Christmas, and within five minutes of meeting Ed, Will and I had established he was mad about cricket too. We told him about the Boxing Day test, driving through the night to get there, armchairs and what have you, and he was instantly hooked. When we got to Wellington our room at our friends place in Willis Street had become a furniture storage room as several flatmates had left, abandoning couches and beds when they did so... So, the Cricket Watching Chair had company that year in the form of a couch and a coffee table and a three legged ashtray. We made the front page of the Evening Post that year under the headline of "Cricket fans watch test in style". Ed was thrilled... he'd been here less than two weeks and he was on the front page of a major daily newspaper. He bought 15 copies and mailed them back to friends in the UK. During that test match we met Phaidra the 17 year old mud wrestler from Featherston (just north of Wellington). She had an unfortunate way with words... she was going back to do her last year of high school the following year. She wanted to be head girl. We said we liked head girls...

It was during the 2000 Boxing Day test at the Basin that we saw Trevor Madondo play his third, and unfortunately what would be his last test match. As had become traditional, we were pretty vocal throughout the test. The Basin scoreboard was having trouble finding enough R's for all the players names, so Andy Flower was on the board for quite a long period of time as 'Andy Flowe'. Many choruses of "Andy Flower's got no R, got no R, got no R, Poor old Andy" to the tune of London Bridge were heard. Brian Strang was bowling into a gale force northerly, and we were heckling him about being so fast. After several shouts of "Give him a faster ball Brian", Ed yelled out "Show him your slower ball!"... and he did and bowled the batsman, and joyously turned to where we were sitting and bowed, causing the whole bank to erupt in laughter.

Trevor Madondo was a joy to watch. He was the first black man to play test cricket for Zimbabwe as a batsman. He was like an antelope in the field and ALWAYS smiling, clearly loving playing test cricket. He never refused to sign an autograph for the kids when fielding on the boundary, and whenever we shouted "Trevor, Trevor give us a smile" he'd turn and flash his brilliant white teeth at us. We sung his name over and over as he batted... In Zimbabwe's first innings he scored his top score in test cricket, 74 not out, and we gave him a standing ovation when he got his 50, which he acknowledged with another brilliant smile and a wave.

So, it was with great sadness that we heard the news in June 2001 that Trevor Madondo had died of malaria in Zimbabwe. We decided that we would build a banner to honour Trevor, and the way he played his cricket, and would take it with us to the Basin every year. Will and I painted the banner in the week before the 2001 Basin Reserve Boxing Day test against Bangladesh. It reads:

TREVOR MADONDO FAN CLUB 74 NOT OUT R.I.P.

Since then, the couches, the Cricket Watching Chair, the coffee table and the chilly bin have been at the Basin under the banner of the Trevor Madondo Fan Club. There are now 6 regulars and more and more of our friends are planning on joining us in 2002.

Brandon and the crew.

Brandon (left) relaxes in a chair while Ed (right) goes the whole hog on the sofa-bed

Not a bad view of the Basin Reserve, is it?

This article first appeared in issue three of the Corridor of Uncertainty
(May 2002)

****

When Leek cricket club faced Checkly in the North Staffs and South Cheshire league young opening bowler Rob Mozalowski found himself bowling to one of the games most recognisable and experienced batsman.

Kim Barnett, ex-opening batsmen for Derbyshire and Gloucestershire, is now playing premier league cricket for Checkly.

Rob as a fan of the game knew who he would be facing and was concerned at how he would deal with Barnett's unusual batting stance. He believed his fears were unfounded after his first two overs but in the end experience won the day over youthful exuberance.

I knew I would be bowling at Kim and from seeing him so many times on TV I knew how he batted, I was nervous but in my second over I ran in to bowl and he edged me through the slips. This gave me the encouragement to put a little bit more into my bowling.

Next over I charged in and took his edge again, this time the ball flew to our keeper but he dropped it. I decided to walk down the wicket and have a word. I said ' Professional? I don't think so anymore.'

The very next ball I put a bouncer in to test him against the short ball. I think to this day the ball is still travelling the hit that he gave it.

Later that innings Barnett added to this six by scoring another nine, in succession.

Rob Mozalowki, Northants 2nd team bowler

****

John Holder has stood in 11 Test matches and has been involved in the game of cricket since his first class playing debut in 1968. His first test match as an umpire was at Lord's in 1988 with England playing Sri Lanka. Robin Smith and Alan Lamb were at the wicket after England had bowled Sri Lanka out cheaply on day one. John continues the story.

"England were batting and batting well. We were nearing the close of the second days play and Robin Smith and Alan Lamb were at the wicket when the light started to fade.

"Alan Lamb has always been one of the great characters of the game; he is a lot of fun and full of mischief.

"With the light getting worse together with David Constant, my umpiring partner, we decided to offer the light to the batsmen which they turned down.

"Half an hour went by and the light had gone from dark to pitch black. As umpires, we only offer the light once to the batsmen and then it is down to them to appeal to us to go off the field.

"They did and Lamb as senior spokesman said: ' Gentleman, I have no problem seeing the ball in this light but I cannot see John Holder at square leg, all I can see is this ghostly white coat.'

"We all fell about laughing and it shows that even in the intensity of a Test match you can enjoy yourself with the players and have a laugh."

John Holder, First Class Umpire (Interviewed by James Holmwood)

Southend Sunday XI v Buckhurst Hill Sunday XI

Southend are batting, poorly. They are 30 odd for the loss of four wickets and Buckhurst Hill has just introduced their front line spin bowler.

A young batsmen named Chris Chambers is heading for the wicket. The lad is known for having every shot in the book but his downfall is that he usually picks the wrong shot most of the time. Today was no exception.

Under orders from the Southend captain to support the batsmen who has been at the wicket for some time Chris takes guard at the crease.

He hangs around for a few overs when the Buckhurst Hill captain makes a fielding change. He adds a second slip in expectation of an edge from Chris's bat, but what he got was something he could not even have imagined.

The wily old spin bowler runs up to bowl and has given the ball some extra loop. Chris has seen this and for some unknown reason has attempted to play the reverse sweep, a shot designed to infuriate opposition captains, as the ball goes the opposite way to that of a regular sweep and into an unguarded area behind the wicket keeper.

Unfortunately for Southend the ball has gone straight into the hands of the newly installed 2nd slip and Southend are five wickets down.

Chris said: "To this day I have no idea why I played that shot, I cannot play a regular sweep shot, let alone a reverse one!"

Chris Chambers, Southend-on-Sea Cricket Club Member

Third and fourth team cricket is often put down by those who play at a higher level but some of the best times you can have take place in these sides.

You will always find the veteran batsmen who seems to have been opening the batting since the club began, the ex-first eleven player who has just had his first child and his wife will only let him play once every month and the bright young thing in the club.

The members of these teams are all good honest people who enjoy being part of a team and the camaraderie that the game brings to their lives.

Sometimes though these players get a little too carried away and their excitement can lead to the downfall of their team mates.

Southend-on-Sea 3rd XI v........... 3 XI

Southend have just bowled their opposition out with pace bowler Roger Walcott taking his first five wicket haul for the club.

In the same side a Comical West Country batsman called Pete Kenton suggests Roger marks this achievement with a souvenir. Tongue in cheek, Pete tells Roger that he should take one of the stumps home to remind him of this performance.

Nobody thinks anymore of this remark until the following week when Southend's captain, who prides himself on his organisational skills, strides to the newly cut strip to place the stumps into the ground. To his horror he finds that there are only five stumps in the kit bag and with the game being played at a park pitch there is no replacement stump on site.

He begins to panic and is also questioning himself as to where the stump could be.

Then last weeks hero walks through the door. Did Roger really take the stump to remind him of his first five wicket haul in the third team of a local cricket league? Nobody dares to ask him as it would be silly to even think that someone would take a souvenir of a third team match In fact it would be stupid to believe anybody would do such a thing in any club side.

Pete, who fears he could be partly to blame for the missing stump, walks over to Roger who does not know the problem the side has and is asked quietly by Pete if he enjoyed last week's performance.

Without a thought for what he has done Roger loudly announces it was the best game of his life and thanks Pete for the idea of a souvenir stump that is now sitting proudly on top of his television set for everyone to see!

James Holmwood, England

Printed in the United Kingdom
by Lightning Source UK Ltd.
110108UKS00001B/4-21